VE LO QUE DICES

See What You Say

Modismos en español e inglés

Spanish and English Idioms

Nancy María Grande Tabor

Charlesbridge

To my mother, Thelma, my colleague, Dr. Martita, and my editor, Yolanda, for making me conscious of the enchantment, meaning, and value of words in three completely different ways.

Thank you most of all to Brent Farmer and Charlesbridge, who make it possible for me to share my words.

—N. T.

The idioms in this book come from different regions of the Spanish-speaking world. Many idioms will be understood by any Spanish speaker, but several will be familiar only to a speaker from a specific region.

Please visit our web page (www.charlesbridge.com/idioms.htm) for a list of more idioms. If you know other Spanish and English idiom pairs, please write to us at the address below or email us at idioms@charlesbridge.com.

Published by Charlesbridge Publishing
85 Main Street, Watertown, MA 02472
(617) 926-0329
www.charlesbridge.com

Printed in South Korea
(sc) 10 9 8 7 6 5 4 3 2 1

The illustrations in this book were done in cut paper.
The display type and text type were set in Korinna.
Digital photographs by Jim Lundell Photography
Printed and bound by Sung In Printing, Inc.,
South Korea
Production supervision by Brian G. Walker
Designed by Diane M. Earley

Library of Congress Cataloging-in-Publication Data
Tabor, Nancy María Grande.
    See what you say/Nancy María Grande Tabor.
        p.   cm.
    Summary: Demonstrates the different ways people
look at the same situations by presenting contrasting
idiomatic expressions in both English and Spanish.
Example: Someone important is a "big wheel" in English
but a "fat fish" in Spanish.
    ISBN 1-57091-376-5 (softcover)
    1. English language—Idioms Juvenile literature.
2. Spanish language—Grammar, Comparative—English
Juvenile literature. 3. English language—Grammar,
Comparative—Spanish Juvenile literature. 4. Spanish
language—Idioms Juvenile literature. [1. English language—
Idioms. 2. Spanish language—Grammar, Comparative—
English. 3. English language—Grammar, Comparative—
Spanish. 4. Spanish language—Idioms.] I. Title
PE1460.T27   2000
428.2'461—dc21   99-19331

¿Qué ves?

What do you see?

¿Ves caras o ves copas? Hay más
de una manera de mirar un cuadro.

Do you see faces, or do you see vases?
There is more than one way to look at a picture.

También hay más de una manera para expresar lo que quieres decir. A veces, el verdadero significado de lo que dices es completamente diferente de las palabras que utilizas. Cuando ocurre, las palabras se llaman un *modismo*.

There is also more than one way to say what you mean. Sometimes the real meaning of what you say is something completely different from the words you use. When this happens, the words are called an *idiom*.

Por ejemplo, puedes decir en español
que "está lloviendo a cántaros,"

For instance, you might say it
is "raining by jugs" in Spanish

o en inglés que "están lloviendo gatos y perros,"
para indicar que está lloviendo con mucha fuerza.

or "raining cats and dogs" in
English if it is raining very hard.

Cuando quieres algo que no puedes tener, puedes decir en español que "la gallina de la vecina pone más huevos que la mía"

When you want something you cannot have, you might say in Spanish that "the neighbor's hen lays more eggs than mine"

y en inglés que "el pasto es siempre
más verde en el otro lado de la cerca."

and in English that "the grass is always
greener on the other side of the fence."

En español "empiezas la casa por el tejado,"

In Spanish you are "starting to build the house at the roof,"

y en inglés "pones la carreta antes que el caballo" cuando haces algo en el orden incorrecto.

and in English you are "putting the cart before the horse" when you do something out of order.

¿Alguien se está burlando de tí? Si sucede eso, entonces en español "está tomándote el pelo,"

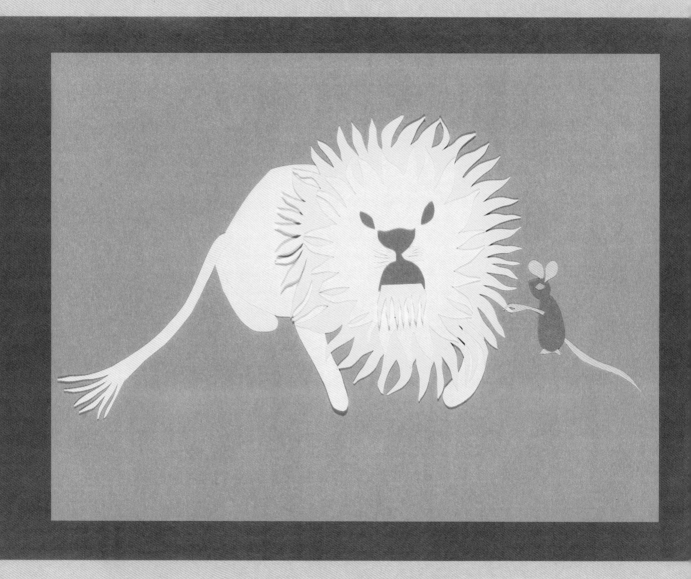

Is someone teasing you? If so, then in Spanish they are "pulling your hair,"

y en inglés "está tirándote de la pierna."

and in English they are "pulling your leg."

Ya sea que en español "eches magaritas a los puercos,"

Whether in Spanish you "throw daisies to the pigs"

o en inglés "eches perlas a los cerdos," de ninguna de las dos maneras la gente aprecia los esfuerzos realizados.

or in English you "cast pearls before swine,"
either way your efforts are not appreciated.

Cuando una persona hace algo sobresaliente,
en español ella "se lleva la palma"

When someone does something outstanding,
in Spanish they "carry off the palm leaf,"

y en inglés "toma el pastel."

and in English they "take the cake."

Cuando es muy fácil hacer algo, se dice que "es más fácil que beber un vaso de agua" en español,

When something is really easy to do, it is "easier than drinking a glass of water" in Spanish

o "tan fácil como caerse de un tronco" en inglés.

or "as easy as falling off a log" in English.

Alguien importante es un "pez gordo" en español

Someone important is a "fat fish" in Spanish

o una "rueda grande" en inglés.

or a "big wheel" in English.

Ya sea que "eches leña al fuego" en español,

Whether you "throw wood on the fire" in Spanish

o "añadas combustible a las llamas" en inglés, estás empeorando lo que ya está mal.

or "add fuel to the flames" in English, you are making matters worse than they already are.

Si alguien no presta atención, en español esa persona "está en la luna"

If someone is not paying attention, in Spanish they are "on the moon,"

y en inglés "tiene su cabeza por las nubes."

and in English they "have their head in the clouds."

En español no quieres encontrarte
"entre la espada y la pared,"

You do not want to find yourself "between
the sword and the wall" in Spanish

o en inglés "entre el diablo y el mar azul profundo," porque eso significa que estás atrapado en una situación sin salida.

or "between the devil and the deep blue sea" in English because it means you have no way out of a situation.

Estás "durmiéndote en las pajas" en español

You are "sleeping in the straw" in Spanish

y estás "dejando que la hierba crezca debajo de tus pies" en inglés, cuando dejas pasar demasiado tiempo para hacer algo.

or "letting the grass grow under your feet" in English when you take too much time to do something.

Cuando se trata de idiomas, nada es "blanco y negro" como dirías en español,

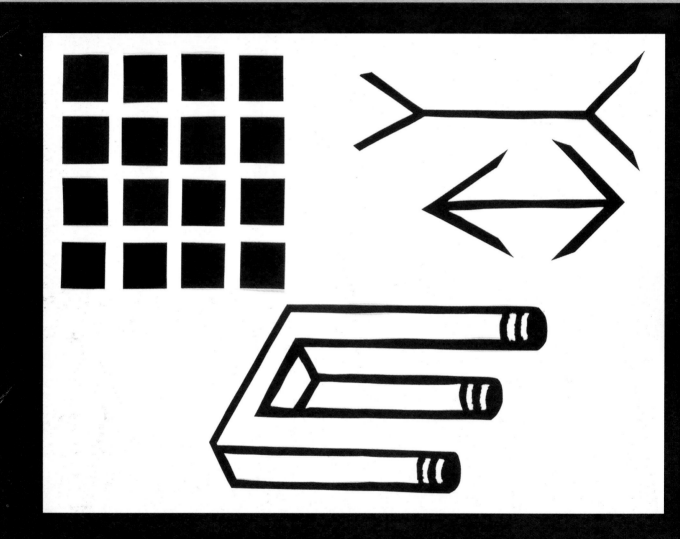

When it comes to language, nothing is "white and black," as you say in Spanish, o "negro y blanco," como dirías en inglés. Hay muchas maneras diferentes de ver y decir las cosas, sea cual sea el idioma que hablas.

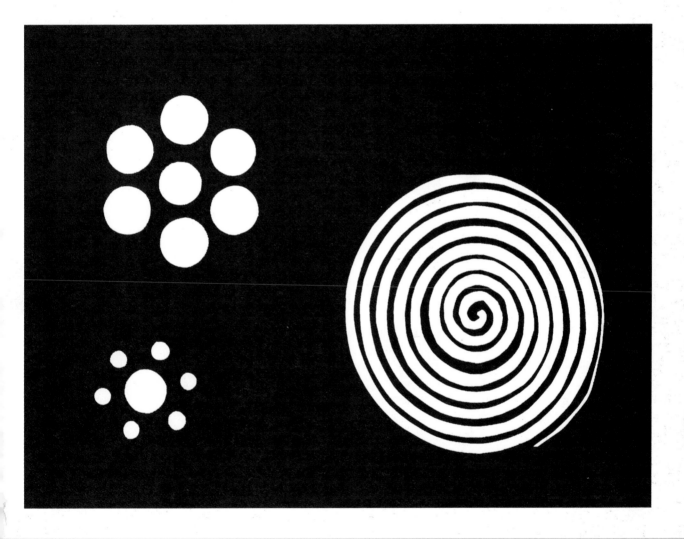

or "black and white," as you say in English. There are many different ways to see and say things, whatever language you speak.

¿No crees que es divertido ver lo que dices?

Isn't it fun to see what you say?